THE WORLD ALMANAC®

BIG PUZZLE CHALLENGE

World Almanac books may be purchased in bulk at special discounts for sales promotion, corporate gifts, fund-raising, or educational purposes. Special editions can also be created to specifications. For details, contact the Special Sales Department, 307 West 36th Street, 11th Floor, New York, NY 10018 or info@skyhorsepublishing.com.

Published by World Almanac, an imprint of Skyhorse Publishing, Inc., 307 West 36th Street, 11th Floor, New York, NY 10018.

The World Almanac® is a registered trademark of Skyhorse Publishing, Inc. All rights reserved.

www.skyhorsepublishing.com

10 9 8 7 6 5 4 3 2 1

Cover design by Melissa Gerber
Cover photographs by Shutterstock
Content, design and typesetting by QualiƷre
www.qualibrecreatives.com

Library of Congress Cataloging-in-Publication Data is available on file.

ISBN: 978-1-5107-7594-7

Printed in China

THE WORLD ALMANAC®

BIG PUZZLE

CHALLENGE

≥ 70 ≤

EXTRA-FUN GAMES AND ACTIVITIES FOR KIDS!

WORLD ALMANAC BOOKS

Contents

Snow Much Fun

Find these 11 objects in the picture. Hint: The objects can change color!

FUN FACT

At an elevation of 14,764–15,420 feet (4,500–4,700 meters) above sea level, Jade Dragon Snow Mountain in the Yunnan province of China is one of the highest ski resorts in the world. Why the name? Some people say it looks like a huge snow-covered dragon!

Penguin Pals

Puffy the royal penguin found a rock he'd like to give to his mate, Penny, to help her build a nest. Can you help Puffy find his way through the maze to Penny?

FUN FACT

The smallest of all penguins are little penguins. Also known as blue penguins, because of their blue and white feathers, they are found in New Zealand, as well as in Australia, where they are called fairy penguins.

London: Seeing Red

Can you spot 8 differences in the pictures below?

FUN FACT

From the national flag, to telephone booths, mailboxes, the uniforms of guards outside Buckingham Palace, to the ever famous double-decker bus, you will definitely "see red" when you visit London.

Tracking African Rivers

Africa is a land of many rivers. Find these 10 important rivers in the word search. The words may run in any direction: forward, backward, diagonally, up, or down.

Nile
Congo
Zambezi
Niger
Limpopo
Okavango
Shebelle
Orange
Kasai
Senegal

O	Z	A	C	L	N	N	R	O	K
K	A	S	A	I	C	I	B	N	L
A	M	D	R	M	Q	L	G	E	O
V	B	X	N	P	M	E	O	E	B
A	E	V	C	O	N	G	O	K	R
N	Z	R	E	P	T	W	Z	C	B
G	I	T	X	O	R	A	N	G	E
O	W	Z	E	S	V	O	I	A	M
S	H	E	B	E	L	L	E	B	A
U	N	L	A	G	E	N	E	S	M

FUN FACT

The two main tributaries of the Nile get their names from the color of the sediment in their waters. The White Nile is rich in light-gray sediment, while the shorter Blue Nile has a darker color because of the black sediment it carries with it.

Hard Facts About Rocks

Read the clue and see if you know which rock is being described. If you don't know, it's written backward for you! Write it correctly on the line and add it to the chart below.

1. I am a soft and white sedimentary rock formed from the shells of marine animals. I am KLAHC _____

2. I am a metamorphic rock found in different colors, but mainly white. I'm used to make statues and sculptures. I am ELBRAM _____

3. I am igneous and one of the hardest rocks. I was used to make the pedestal of the Statue of Liberty. I am ETINARG _____

4. I have light gray and white bands. I'm metamorphic, and my name is pronounced "nice." I am SSIENG _____

5. I am an igneous rock, and I'm also found on the moon. I am TLASAB _____

Igneous

_____
_____
_____
_____

Metamorphic

_____
_____
_____
_____

Sedimentary

_____
_____
_____
_____

Twin Dragons

Find the two identical dragons and draw a line between them.

FUN FACT

A dragon is a mythical creature that could fly and spit fire from its mouth. While the yellow and orange flag of Bhutan has a white dragon on it, the Welsh flag has a red dragon. Wales, along with England and Scotland, is a part of Great Britain.

Tulip TOWN

Can you spot 8 differences in the pictures below?

FUN FACT

Colorful tulips are known to have originated not from the Netherlands but from Turkey and Central Asia, where they grew wild! Their shape was responsible for their name. It comes from the word *Tulipan* which means turban!

Tunneling Through

Help the mole find his way to the sumptuous earthworm pie that's waiting for him.

FUN FACT

Moles are small animals that spend most of their lives underground, creating tunnels and pathways through soil. As they dig, they discard excavated soil at the surface, forming typical "molehills." They love earthworms and a single mole can eat up to 200 worms a day!

Desert Dwellers

Desert animals are well-adapted to life in the desert. Find 10 animals in the word search that consider this habitat their home. The words may run in any direction: forward, backward, diagonally, up, or down.

A	R	M	A	D	I	L	L	O	X
C	E	E	B	B	R	J	T	A	O
A	S	E	O	C	D	D	C	H	F
S	T	R	L	X	L	E	M	A	C
A	A	K	L	E	E	D	I	J	E
N	N	A	I	X	N	C	D	E	N
D	A	T	U	A	N	A	T	R	N
C	U	R	T	D	J	E	X	B	E
A	G	X	A	D	M	G	I	O	F
T	I	B	B	A	R	K	C	A	J

Armadillo
Bat
Jackrabbit
Iguana
Meerkat
Sand Cat
Jerboa
Fennec Fox
Addax
Camel

FUN FACT

Jackrabbits are not really rabbits but hares. What's the difference? Rabbits are born with no fur, and they live in burrows; hares are born with fur, and they live in nests above the ground.

Marsupial Surprise

Use the color codes to reveal a special kind of animal in its favorite spot.

FUN FACT

Often referred to as koala bears, cuddly koalas are not bears but marsupials, mammals who carry their little ones in a pouch. They can sleep for hours in their favorite spot—in a eucalyptus tree!

Castles and More Castles!

Find two identical castles and draw a line between them.

FUN FACT

While Germany tops the list as the country with the greatest number of castles, Wales, a country that is part of the United Kingdom, has more castles per square mile.

Under the Sea

Can you spot 8 differences in the pictures below?

FUN FACT

Beautiful, colorful coral reefs that are home to a variety of marine life are turning white because of the warming of ocean waters. This is called coral bleaching. Coral Reef Alliance (CORAL) is one of the largest organizations working to protect coral reefs across the globe.

Capital Clue

I'm an important location in the world. I'm a national capital. Read the clue and guess which capital I am. If you don't know, it's written backward for you! Write it correctly on the line.

1. I am the capital of Canada, the country with the most natural lakes.
   AWATTO _____

2. My country, France, is proud of its Eiffel Tower. **SIRAP** _____

3. Looking to go on a wildlife safari? Visit my country, Kenya. **IBORIAN** _____

4. You would love to see the cherry blossoms bloom in my country, Japan.
   OYKOT _____

5. I am the capital of Germany. I was once partitioned into East and West.
   NILREB _____

6. My country, India, is famous for its numerous festivals. **IHLED** _____

7. My country, Russia, is the largest in the world. **WOCSOM** _____

8. Longing to see kangaroos? Stop over in my country, Australia.
   ARREBNAC _____

Pyramid Puzzler

Look at the pyramid made of colored pencils and identify the correct top view.

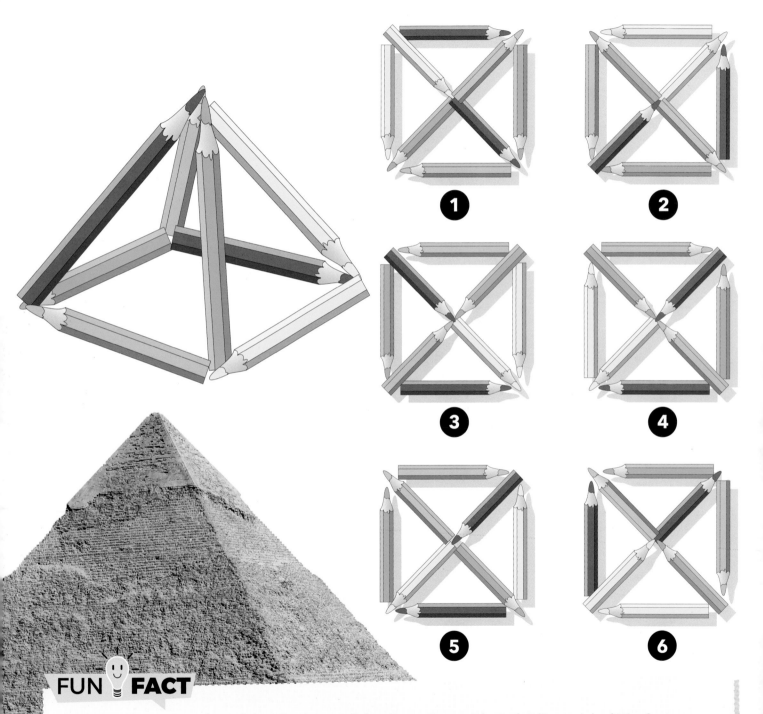

FUN FACT

Scientists have now found that the base of the Great Pyramid, or the Pyramid of Khufu, is not a perfect square. The west side is slightly longer than the east. Of the many pyramids in Egypt, the largest, the Great Pyramid of Giza, is the only Wonder of the Ancient World that is still standing.

Island Discovery

There are some amazing islands in the Mediterranean Sea. Find 10 of them in the word search. The words may run in any direction: forward, backward, diagonally, up, or down.

S	E	D	O	H	R	C	A	Z	B
I	Y	D	I	N	S	O	L	A	I
C	A	P	R	I	A	R	M	R	N
I	B	I	Z	A	R	S	H	D	I
L	A	S	O	S	D	I	C	P	R
Y	R	U	N	C	I	C	A	S	O
Z	D	R	I	Y	N	A	O	R	T
A	I	P	T	L	I	M	C	P	N
M	Y	Y	Z	M	A	L	T	A	A
D	E	C	R	E	T	E	M	R	S

Sicily
Sardinia
Santorini
Rhodes
Ibiza
Malta
Crete
Corsica
Capri
Cyprus

FUN FACT

Sicily, one of the largest islands in the Mediterranean Sea, is surrounded by three seas: the Mediterranean Sea in the south, the Tyrrhenian Sea in the north, and the Ionian Sea in the east.

Culture Cats

Color this picture of a cat in Ancient Egypt.

FUN FACT

Ancient Egyptians believed in a goddess named Bastet who could turn herself into a cat.

Let's Go Dinosauring!

Help the dino find its way to the egg.

FUN FACT

What's a clutch? It's the number of eggs laid by a female dinosaur at one time. Depending upon the species, dinosaurs laid 1 to 5 eggs; some laid as many as 20 at a time.

Let's Celebrate

All around the world, people celebrate their unique holidays and hold exciting festivals. Find the names of 10 important days and festivals in the word search. The words may run in any direction: forward, backward, diagonally, up, or down.

O	K	T	O	B	E	R	F	E	S	T
H	A	M	C	U	M	S	T	O	O	C
A	H	A	L	L	O	W	E	E	N	H
N	E	W	Y	E	A	R	O	D	G	R
U	C	B	H	I	E	M	A	I	K	I
K	Y	I	P	E	N	G	N	W	R	S
K	S	D	N	H	B	A	B	A	A	T
A	H	N	D	B	O	O	E	L	N	M
H	E	T	A	B	P	L	S	I	C	A
L	A	T	O	M	A	T	I	N	A	S
O	J	O	U	T	E	S	R	T	A	S

CHRISTMAS
SONGKRAN
DIWALI
NEW YEAR
HALLOWEEN
OKTOBERFEST
HANUKKAH
LA TOMATINA
HOLI
YI PENG

FUN FACT

People who left England and Ireland and went to America in the 1800s brought their Halloween traditions with them, with one key change. Instead of making lanterns out of carved turnips, they started using pumpkins.

Let It Snow

What unique item is hiding behind these dots? Connect the numbers to find out.

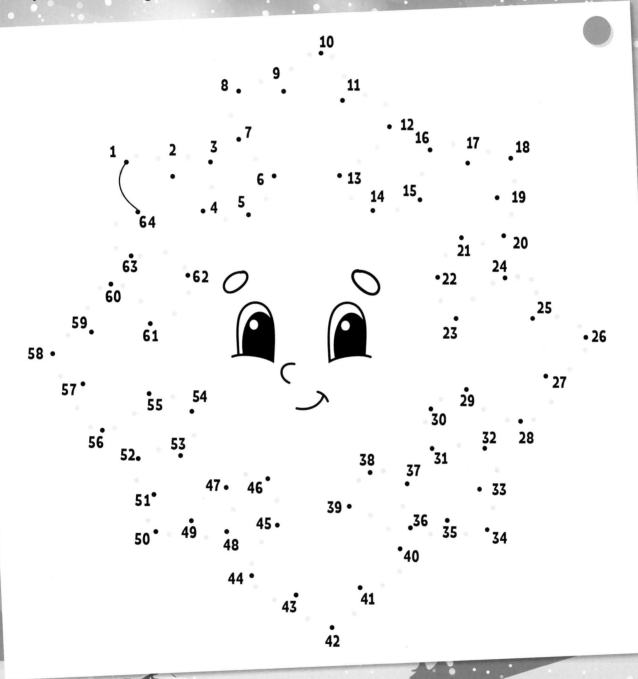

FUN FACT

Some of the snowiest cities in the world are Syracuse in New York; Sapporo in Japan; and Chamonix in France.

Amazing Amazon

The Amazon rain forest is home to more than a thousand species of birds. Find 10 of our flying friends in the word search. The words may run in any direction: forward, backward, diagonally, up, or down.

O	G	T	R	O	U	P	I	A	L
A	R	I	W	A	M	O	G	U	N
T	E	Z	G	U	A	N	F	I	S
H	A	R	P	Y	E	A	G	L	E
I	T	O	O	M	A	C	A	W	Z
Z	E	P	K	I	N	U	E	O	M
N	G	T	A	L	P	O	T	O	O
T	R	O	T	O	M	T	O	M	I
R	E	H	S	I	F	G	N	I	K
M	T	U	N	I	Z	T	A	O	H

Harpy eagle
Toucan
Hoatzin
Macaw
Guan
Potoo
Kingfisher
Motmot
Troupial
Great Egret

FUN FACT

Potoos, with their awesome yellow "googly" eyes, are excellent at camouflage. They sit still for hours on a dead branch with their eyes closed, looking like a part of the branch itself.

Population Boom

Search the busy crowd for the red-headed man with eyeglasses. If you find him, circle him!

FUN FACT

Which age group has the largest population in the world? It's young people between the ages of 10 and 24 years old. About half of the world's population is under 30 years old.

Tree Talk

Read the clue and find the name of the tree in the word box. Write the name on the line.

cacao   maple   cinchona   eucalyptus   oak   baobab

1. My fruit are acorns.

_____

2. Chocolate is produced from my beans.

_____

3. I am often referred to as the "Tree of Life."

_____

4. Koalas love to live on my branches and eat my leaves.

_____

5. Quinine, which is used to treat malaria, is made from my bark.

_____

6. I am a symbol of Canada.

_____

Soccer Time

Can you spot 8 differences in the pictures below?

 **FUN FACT**

The FIFA World Cup was held in the months of November and December for the first time in 2022 because of the extreme high temperatures in summer in Qatar, the host country. In another first, every stadium had central air conditioning!

23

Vulture Vibes

Help these vultures follow the branches back to their chicks.

FUN FACT

Vultures aren't noisy birds. They mostly just growl or hiss. They have an amazing digestive system, so even though they are scavengers, they never seem to get food poisoning.

Hoo-Hoo, Who?

**Use the color codes and color by number.
Then find me in the picture.**

FUN FACT

Owls are mysterious birds. They can rotate their heads 270 degrees—almost all the way around. With their tubular eyes and silent flight, these nocturnal birds are amazing hunters.

25

To the Hoop

Help this basketball player dribble his way to the basket.

FUN FACT

Basketball, played all across the globe, was invented in the United States. It is also popular in Australia, the Philippines, Canada, Argentina, and Iraq.

26

Flightless Birds

I'm a bird, but I can't fly. Who am I? My name is written backward. Write it correctly on the line provided.

1. OPAKAK _____

2. YRAWOSSAC _____

3. HCIRTSO _____

4. IWIK _____

5. NIUGNEP _____

6. AEHR _____

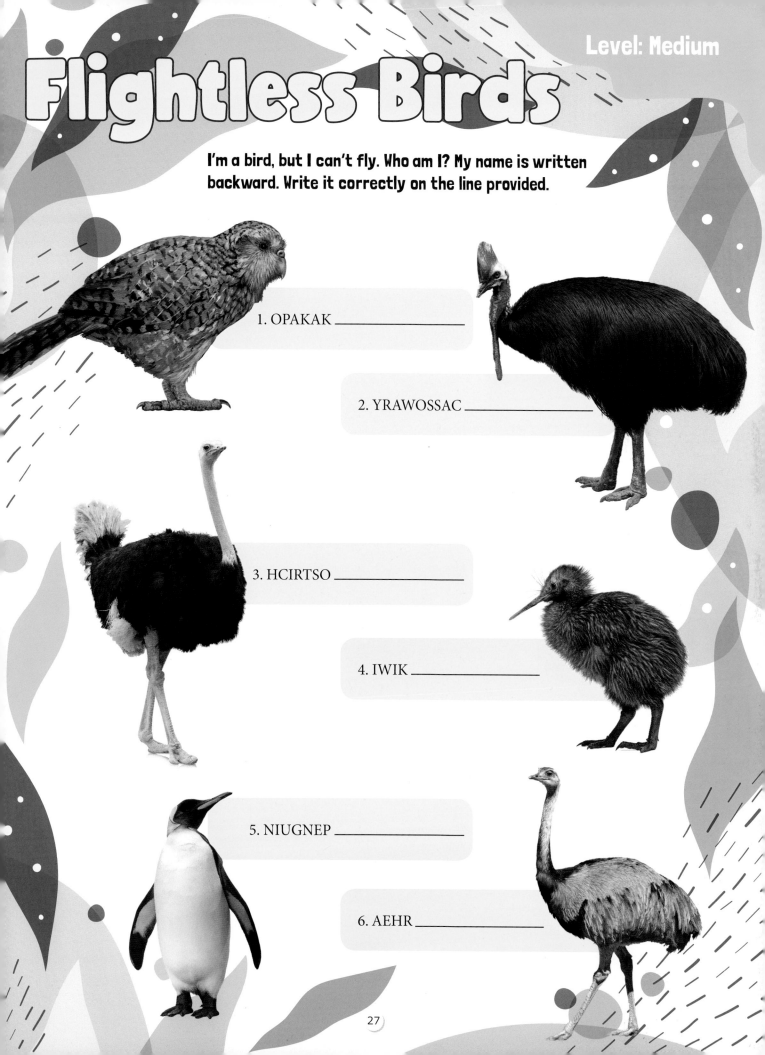

Chasing Waterfalls

No two waterfalls are the same; each has its own unique identity. Find the names of 10 famous waterfalls in the word search. The words may run in any direction; forward, backward, diagonally, up, or down.

E	N	I	H	R	S	T	A	N	Y
K	A	I	E	T	E	U	R	I	A
A	B	D	T	S	E	G	R	G	I
I	A	G	I	S	V	E	G	U	H
R	A	R	M	O	I	L	K	A	E
O	Y	O	E	F	C	A	L	Z	N
T	E	S	S	L	O	L	E	U	W
C	G	M	O	L	S	M	G	A	O
I	E	I	Y	U	S	E	N	S	R
V	N	I	A	G	A	R	A	I	B

Angel
Victoria
Niagara
Yosemite
Iguazu
Gullfoss
Kaieteur
Tugela
Rhine
Browne

FUN FACT

Named after famous aviator Jimmie Angel, the highest waterfall is Angel Falls. The fall is so high that in summer some of the water is said to evaporate before it touches the ground.

Toadstool Twins

Find two identical sets of mushrooms, also called toadstools, and draw a line between them.

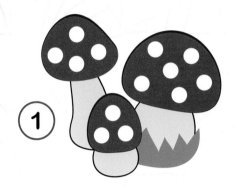 **1**

 **2**

 **3**

 **4**

 **5**

 **6**

 **7**

 **8**

 **9**

FUN FACT

Mushrooms are a type of fungi. While there are many varieties of edible mushrooms, beware of those growing in the wild! They may be pretty, but some of them are extremely poisonous!

Checkmate

Take a look at the game of chess in progress below. Can you identify what the top view looks like?

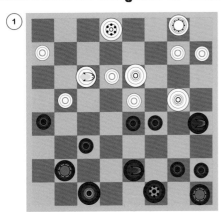
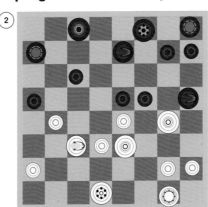
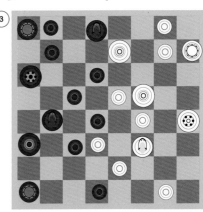
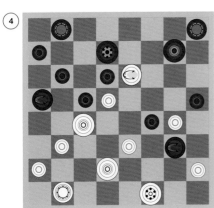
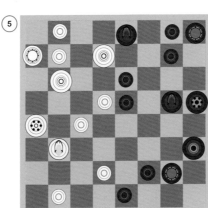
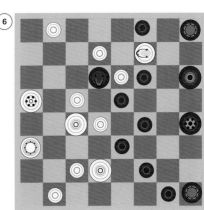

FUN FACT

The word *checkmate* is used in chess when you've "captured" your opponent's king and won the game. It comes from the Persian phrase, "Shah Mat," which translates to, "the king is frozen" or "the king is dead."

Bonding Lemurs

Can you spot 8 differences in the pictures below?

FUN FACT

Ring-tailed lemurs, with white bellies and dark triangular patches around their eyes, have tails with 13 alternating black and white bands. They live in groups and love sunbathing!

It's Bedtime Somewhere

Somewhere in the world, it's bedtime! Find the hidden objects in this picture of a sleepy girl with all her pets. Hint: The objects can change color!

1.
2.
3.
4.
5.
6.
7.
8.
9.
10.

FUN FACT

Sleep on the job? That's exactly what you would have to do if you worked as a "professional sleeper" in one of the hotels in Finland. The job: sleep on a bed and test its quality and comfort!

Bee Patient

Help the bees reach the flower to collect some nectar.

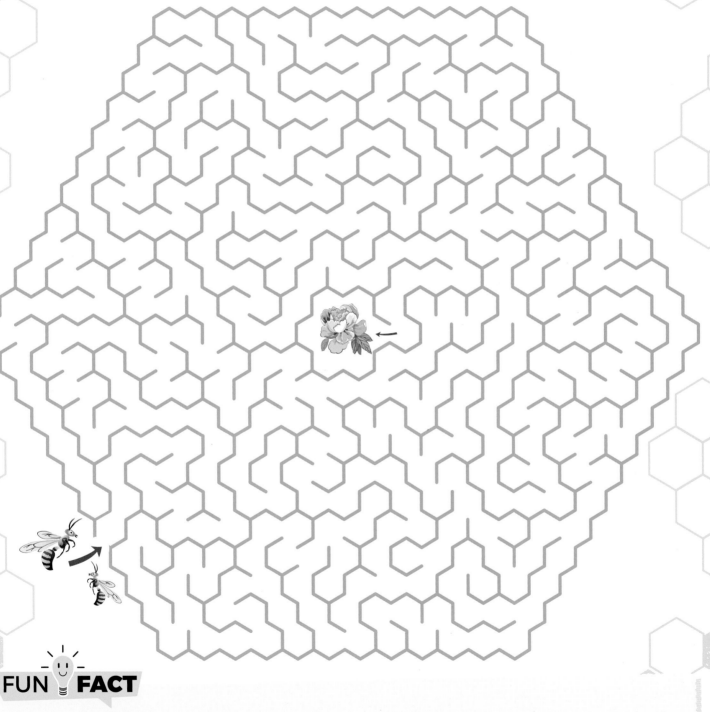

FUN FACT

Bees don't just make honey. They make bread, too! Adult female bees mix pollen with nectar, honey, and a bit of saliva and form bee bread in honeycomb cells for the little ones to feed on.

Currency Quest

Draw a line to match each bill to the country where it is used.

Currency	Country

1.

a. Denmark

2.

b. Japan

3.

c. United States

4.

d. Iraq

5.

e. India

**FUN FACT**

The 10-centimes coin of Switzerland is said to be the oldest original coin still in use. It looks the same as it did in 1879.

Tusky Wally

Use the color codes and color the picture to see what item of clothing Wally is wearing.

1 5

2 6

3 7

4 8

FUN FACT

The tusks that you see on a walrus are actually two canine teeth that turn into tusks of ivory.
In zoos, walruses actually go for regular dental checkups!

Watery Watermelons

Study the watermelon at the center of the puzzle. Circle the child with the missing slice.

FUN FACT

True to its name, a watermelon contains almost 92% water by weight. It also has plenty of seeds. Did you know that the world record distance for watermelon seed spitting is 75 feet, 2 inches?

Entertain Me

Find **10** popular forms of entertainment in the word search below. The words may run in any direction: forward, backward, diagonally, up, or down.

T	R	A	V	E	L	C	N	C	M
H	A	O	U	E	P	I	M	O	O
E	C	O	N	C	E	R	T	S	V
A	C	L	L	X	L	C	O	H	I
T	B	L	U	A	Y	U	C	O	E
E	N	M	D	B	R	S	W	W	S
R	M	N	P	E	S	S	B	S	S
S	T	R	O	P	S	E	A	R	A
R	S	N	M	B	O	O	K	S	B
T	C	A	R	N	I	V	A	L	P

Sports
Movies
Circus
Travel
Concerts
Shows
Books
Clubs
Theater
Carnival

FUN FACT

The first known circus took place in 1768, when Philip Astley, a cavalry officer, showed off his horse riding tricks in an open-air theater in London for a live audience.

Migrating Monarchs

Help this monarch butterfly migrate from the United States to the forests of Mexico.

FUN FACT

How does one identify a monarch butterfly? An adult has two pairs of bright orange-red wings, each with black veins and white spots along the edges. Males are larger, with black dots along their veins.

Flying High

Can you spot 8 differences in the pictures below?

FUN FACT

While most flags are rectangular in shape, the flags of Switzerland ➕ and the Vatican City 🏛️ are squares. Nepal's flag is like two stacked triangles. 🚩

Hungry Pelicans

These pelicans are very hungry. Can you help them find **10** fish hidden in the image below?

FUN FACT

Pelicans are the only birds with a pouch. Their pouches are under their bills, and they use them to catch fish.

The Americas

Look at the cartoon map of North and South America and see if you can find all the pictures at right. Cross them off as you go!

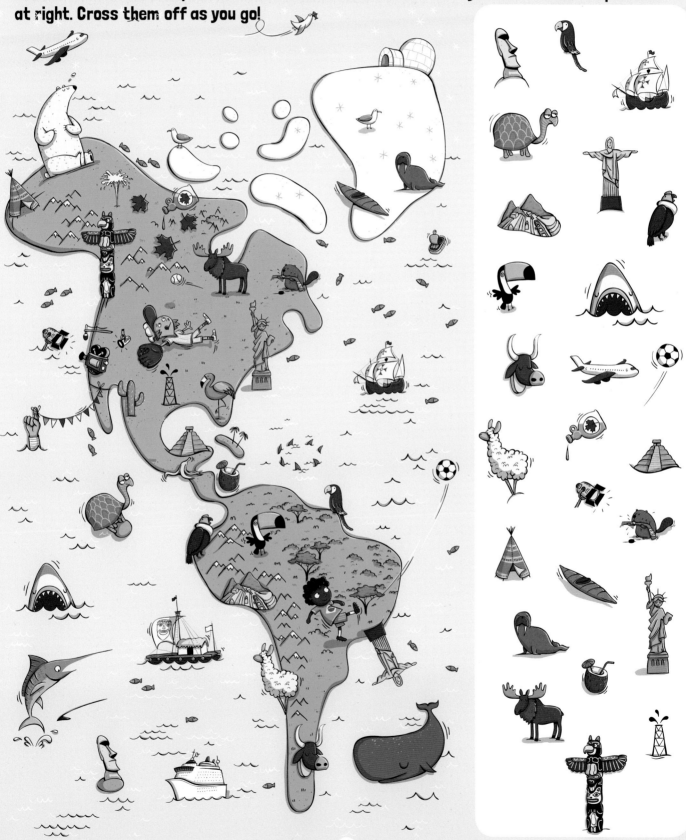

Have a Heart

Match the heart fact to the correct animal.

1. I have multiple hearts and multiple tentacles!

2. My heart rate is super speedy (250 beats per minute), just like me.

3. I'm small, but my heart is a long tube with many chambers.

4. During an underwater dive, my heart rate can go very low.

5. I have no heart, brain, or eyes!

6. When a part of my heart is damaged, I can regenerate it!

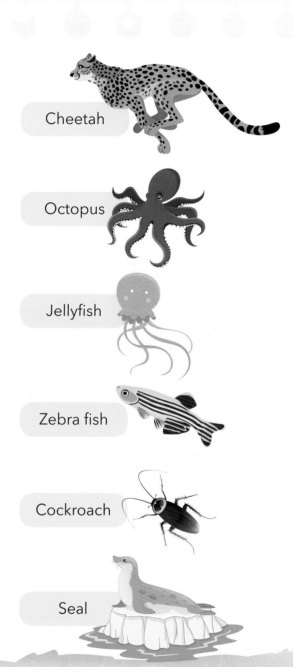

Cheetah

Octopus

Jellyfish

Zebra fish

Cockroach

Seal

 **FUN FACT**

The animal with the smallest heart in the world is a wasp-like insect, the fairy fly. The blue whale has the largest heart.

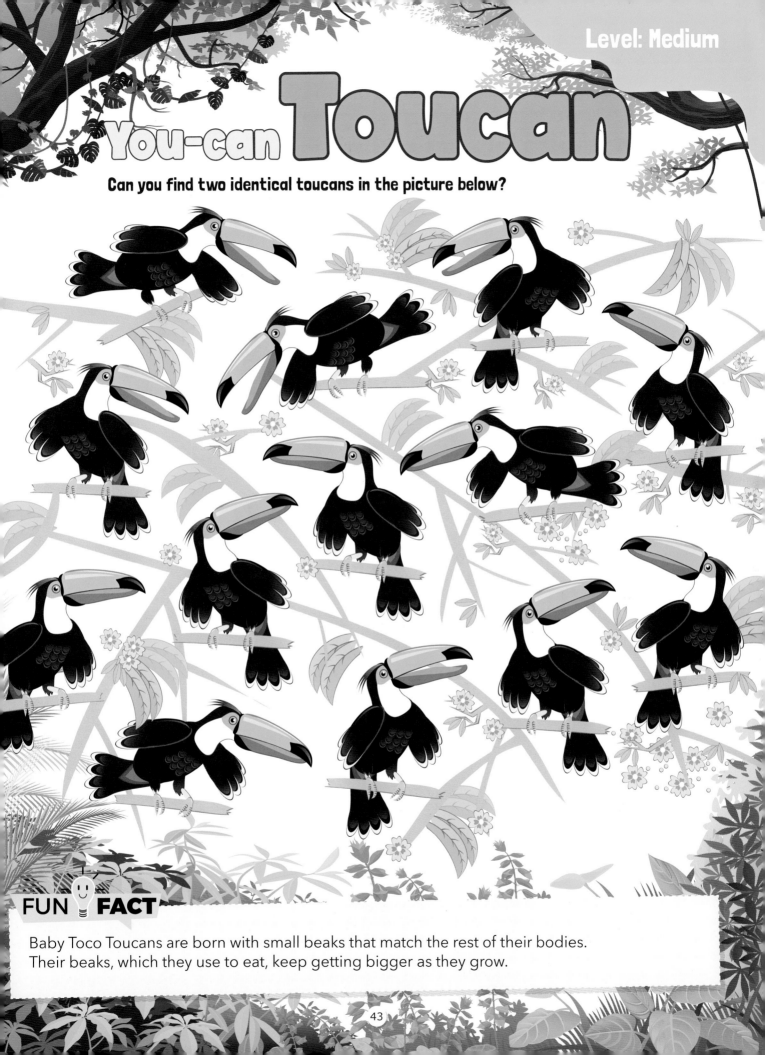

You-can Toucan

Can you find two identical toucans in the picture below?

FUN FACT

Baby Toco Toucans are born with small beaks that match the rest of their bodies.
Their beaks, which they use to eat, keep getting bigger as they grow.

Which Windmill?

Can you find the windmill that is reflected in the lake?

FUN FACT

Some of the oldest windmills in the world are found in Nashtifan, Iran. These windmills were not used to generate electricity but to mill grain to make flour and to pump water.

At the Watering Hole

Animals big and small flock to a watering hole. Can you spot 8 differences in the pictures below?

FUN FACT

Elephants can drink around 26–53 gallons (100–200 liters) of water in a day. They don't use their trunks to drink water, exactly. They fill their trunks up with water and then pour it into their mouths the way you'd use a garden hose.

Related Reptiles

Read the clue and see if you can identify the reptile. Use the word bank and write your best guess on the line.

Crocodile   Alligator   Tortoise   Turtle   Chameleon   Gecko

1.   I have a broad, U-shaped snout, and I'm usually found in fresh water.

_____

2.   I have a narrow, V-shaped snout, and I prefer salt water.

_____

3.   I have a rounded shell, stumpy feet, and I spend most of my time on land.

_____

4.   I have a streamlined shell, flipper-like feet, and I prefer the water.

_____

5.   I am a lizard that can change its color.

_____

6.   I am a small green or brown nocturnal lizard whose color doesn't change.

_____

Claw-some Crustacean

Use the color codes and color by number. Then find me in the picture.

FUN FACT

Their bright red color is what makes the Christmas Island crabs famous all over the world. When they migrate to the Indian Ocean to breed and lay eggs, they look like spectacular "rivers of red."

Spaced Out

Find the 15 objects in the picture. Cross them out as you go.

FUN FACT

Way beyond the clouds, there are thousands and thousands of pieces of space junk flying around. The junk includes bits and pieces of spacecrafts and rockets, and satellites no longer in use!

To Be A Gondolier

Can you spot 8 differences in the pictures below?

FUN FACT

Becoming a gondolier in Venice is not easy. Initially, it was a tradition that was passed down from father to son. Today, you need to be trained and licensed.

A Long Flight

Help this Arctic tern reach Antarctica. Start moving from 1 and follow the numbers in sequence to reach 100.

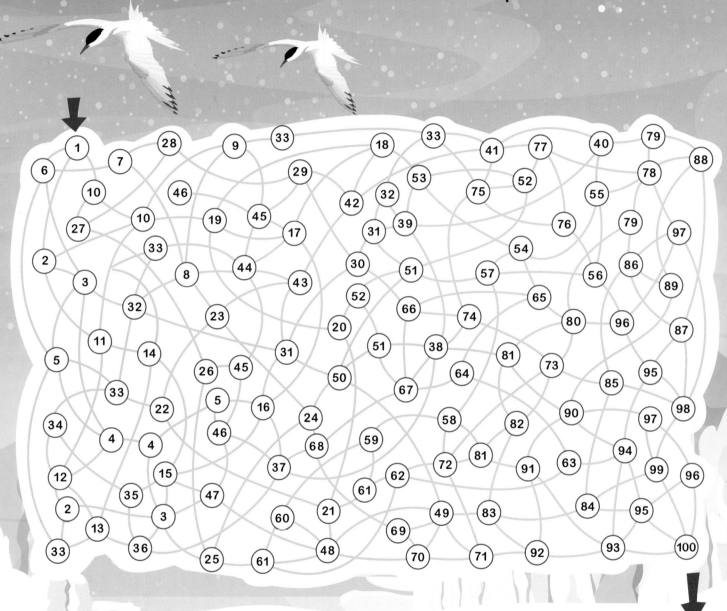

 **FUN FACT**

The Arctic tern is a small migratory bird that spends most of the year flying across the globe from the Arctic to the Antarctic. It's one of the longest migrations on Earth!

Legends Galore

Match the clues about legendary creatures to the correct pictures.

1. I am the Loch Ness monster, an aquatic beast from Scotland.

2. Known as the Yeti, I am the abominable snowman and my legend began in Nepal.

3. I am Kraken, the giant squid from Norway.

4. I am Ogopogo, the lake monster from Canada.

5. I am Sasquatch, commonly known as Bigfoot. I'm from North America.

6. I'm a leprechaun, a tiny man from Ireland who searches for gold at the end of a rainbow.

Chocolate
for the Win

Fill in the missing chocolate pieces to make the bar whole again. Write the number and draw the piece where it belongs on the bar.

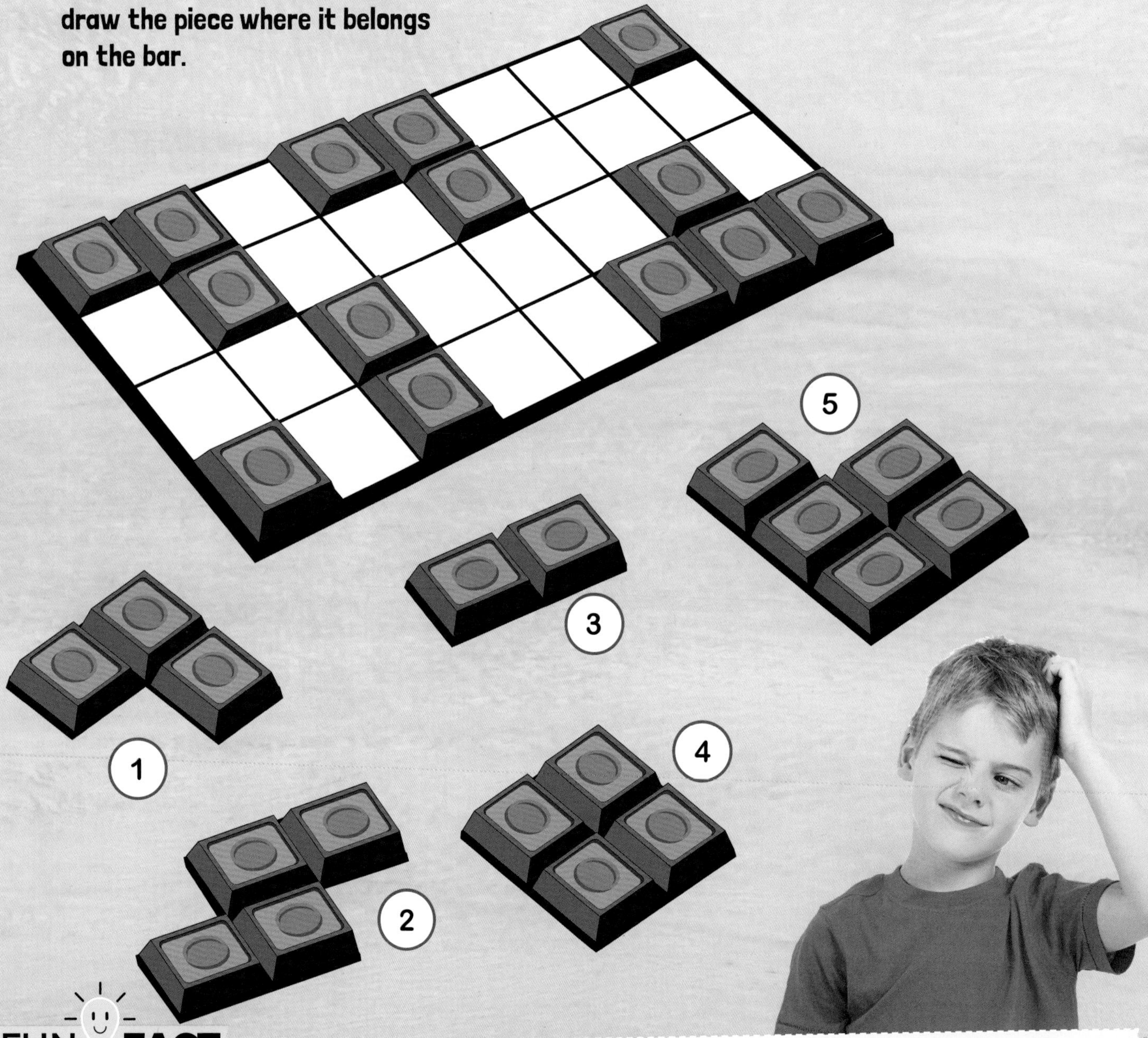

1

2

3

4

5

The ancient Aztecs and Mayans actually used cacao beans, the kind that chocolate is made from, as money. They believed these seeds were given to them by the gods and were very valuable.

World Flags

How well do you know these flags from across the world?
Match the names of the countries to the flags.

 a.

1. Hungary

 b.

2. Netherlands

 c.

3. Armenia

 d.

4. Great Britain

 FUN FACT

Some people say that former British Prime Minister Margaret Thatcher helped invent soft-serve ice cream! After college, she used her chemistry degree to help a food company add air to ice cream and pump it through a machine for kids everywhere to enjoy.

Swooping Magpies

Find two identical magpies and draw a line between them.

FUN FACT

Magpies can recognize people by their faces. If they swoop down on you once, there's a good chance that they will do it again.

Bullet Ant Adventure

Help this bullet ant find its way out of its anthill.

FUN FACT

Found in the forests of Central and South America, the bullet ant is said to have an extremely powerful, painful sting—almost like you've been hit by a bullet.

Flower Finder

Use the color codes and color by number. Then find me in the picture.

FUN FACT

Sunflowers don't just angle their heads toward the sun. They are also "clean-up" agents who help clear the environment of radioactive waste and other toxic materials.

Tiny Books

Look at these piles of knowledge, and identify the correct top view.

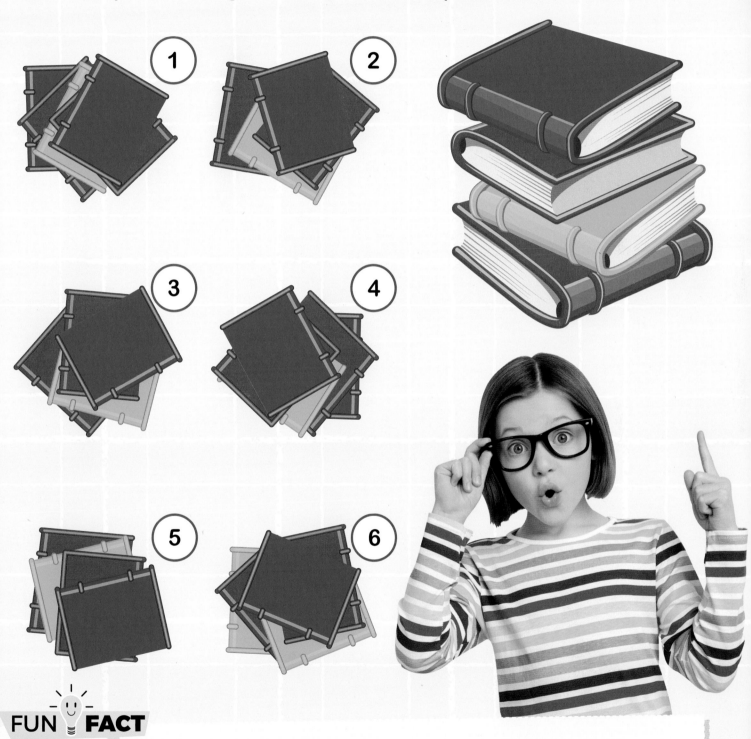

1

2

3

4

5

6

FUN FACT

The record for the smallest book goes to *Teeny Ted From Turnip Town*. How tiny is it? 100 micrometers by 70 micrometers! You need a scanning electron microscope just to read it.

57

Creepy Crawly

Match the clue to the picture of the insect.

1. I glow in the dark. I produce my own light.

2. I'm tough. I could survive a nuclear blast.

3. If I bite you when you're in the woods, you'll likely get an itchy bump.

4. I can jump and jump. I have ears on my belly.

5. I'm cute. I'm brightly colored. I have a spotted dome.

a.

Mosquito

b.

Grasshopper

c.

Cockroach

d.

Ladybug

e.

Firefly

Let's Go Fishing!

Find these **10** objects in the picture below.

FUN FACT

Dolphins are unique in their hunting techniques. From herding their prey to the surface by producing bubbles, to "fish whacking," stunning fish by hitting them, it's fun to watch them catch their meal!

City Tracker

Here are some of the largest cities in the world. Can you match them with the country they belong to?

1. São Paulo   **a.** Sweden

2. Cairo   **b.** Bangladesh

3. Stockholm   **c.** China

4. Dhaka   **d.** Egypt

5. Berlin   **e.** Japan

6. Shanghai   **f.** Afghanistan

7. Tokyo   **g.** Brazil

8. Kabul   **h.** Germany

Mer-maidens

Spot 15 differences in the pictures below.

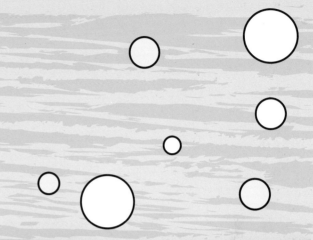

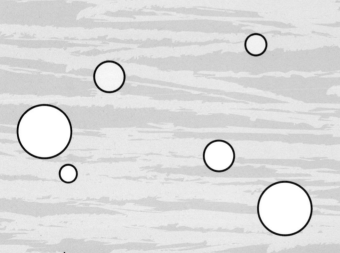

FUN FACT

Do mermaids actually exist? One possible explanation for their sightings could be the gentle manatees also known as sea cows. Sailors may have mistaken them for mermaids.

Street Smart

Find 8 differences on this street in New York.

 FUN FACT

New York, popularly known as "The Big Apple," was not always New York. A long, long time ago when Dutch fur traders first settled there, they called it New Amsterdam.

Monumental Monuments

Match the name of the monument with its picture.

1. **Mount Rushmore**

a.

2. **Liberty Bell**

b.

3. **Lincoln Memorial**

c.

4. **Statue of Liberty**

d.

5. **Washington Monument**

e.

Sea View

Color all the sea creatures in the picture.

FUN FACT

The red octopus found in the Atlantic Ocean has eight arms with glow-in-the-dark suckers. Scientists think they use their glow to attract prey.

To the Top

Level: Medium

Find the numbered path that takes the hiker to the top of the mountain.

FUN FACT

Many mountains today have yet to be conquered. Gangkhar Puensum in Bhutan, near the Tibetan border, is one of the highest unclimbed mountains on Earth.

Autumn Leaves

Autumn is the season of falling leaves and changing colors. Find these 10 objects in the picture.

FUN FACT

In autumn, green leaves change to yellow, orange, red, and even purple. Some of the best places to see fall foliage are Lapland, Finland; New England in the United States; Tuscany, Italy; Jiuzhaigou Valley National Park, China; and Kyoto, Japan.

Dogs From All Over

Find 10 breeds of dogs in the word search. The words may run in any direction: forward, backward, diagonally, up, or down.

Poodle
Retriever
Husky
Pug
Dalmatian
Boxer
Beagle
Doberman
Bulldog
Spaniel

G	O	D	L	L	U	B	R	L	N
R	O	A	E	H	U	S	K	Y	A
E	L	L	A	G	D	A	L	H	M
V	E	M	S	U	G	R	E	B	R
E	I	A	B	H	O	O	X	I	E
I	N	T	E	E	L	G	A	E	B
R	A	I	O	G	X	R	A	P	O
T	P	A	O	U	E	D	B	O	D
E	S	N	M	P	O	O	D	L	E
R	E	X	O	B	A	N	U	Y	H

FUN FACT

Affenpinschers, also known as "monkey terriers," are a breed of very small dogs with faces very much like monkeys. Way back in the 1600s, they were used to hunt rats and other pests in German stables.

Rare and Common Flowers

Some of these bouquets are one of a kind, but two are just the same. Find two identical flower arrangements and draw a line between them.

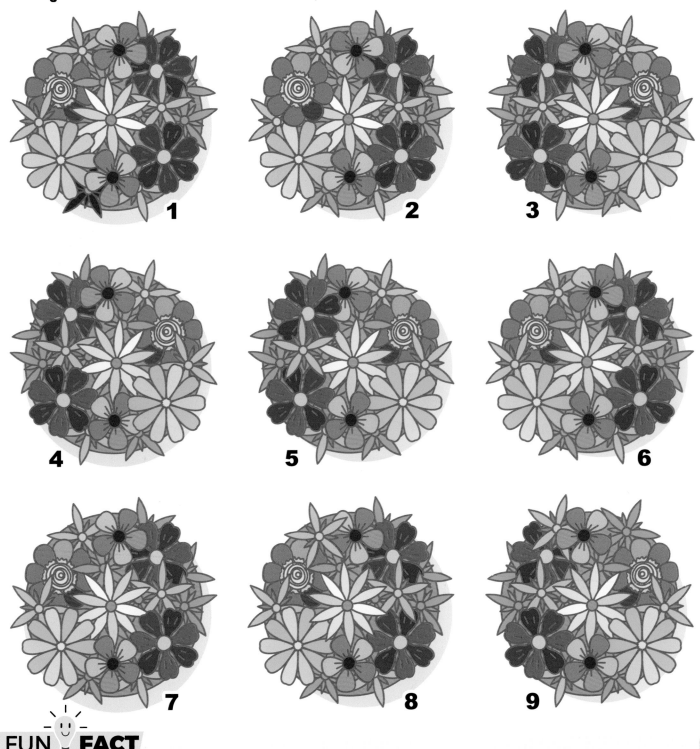

1

2

3

4

5

6

7

8

9

FUN FACT

One of the largest and rarest flowers in the world, the Titan Arum, is also the smelliest! Hold your nose! Native to Sumatra, Indonesia, and referred to as the "corpse flower," it smells like rotting flesh!

Forest Trail

Find these **10** forest dwellers in the picture below. Can you name the forest dwellers?
Hint: Their names are written backward below.

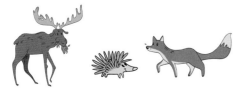

1. GOHEGDEH _____

2. WORC _____

3. LWO _____

4. SEEB _____

5. XOF _____

6. TIBBAR _____

7. ESOOM _____

8. REKCEPDOOW _____

9. LERRIUQS _____

10. GIP _____

A moose is the largest member of the deer family. A male is called a bull moose, while a female is called a cow moose.

Magnificent Harbors

Match these famous harbors to the country or continent where they're found.

1.  Sydney Harbor

    a. Brazil

2.  Neko Harbor

    b. Hong Kong

3.  Rio de Janeiro Harbor

    c. Australia

4.  Victoria Harbor

    d. United States

5.  New York Harbor

    e. Malta

6. Grand Harbor

    f. Antarctica

Sail Away

Find two identical sets of sailboats and draw a line between them.

FUN FACT

The largest ocean on Earth is the Pacific Ocean. It is so large that all the continents of the world could fit inside it.

Answers

Page 1

Page 2

Page 3

Page 4

```
O Z     L N N
K A S A I   I
A M     M   L G
V B     P E   E
A E   C O N G O     R
N Z     P
G I     O R A N G E
O S
S H E B E L L E
  L A G E N E S
```

Page 5

1. CHALK - Sedimentary
2. MARBLE - Metamorphic
3. GRANITF - Igneous
4. GNEISS - Metamorphic
5. BASALT - Igneous

Page 6

7   14

Page 7

Page 8

Page 9

```
A R M A D I L L O X
  E           O
  E           F
S R     L E M A C
A A K         J E
N N A   X     E N
D A T   A     R N
C U   T D     B E
A G   A D     O F
T I B B A R K C A J
```

Page 10

Page 11

12   14

Page 12

Answers

Page 13

1. Ottawa
2. Paris
3. Nairobi
4. Tokyo
5. Berlin
6. Delhi
7. Moscow
8. Canberra

Page 14

Page 15

S	E	D	O	H	R	C			
I				S	O			I	
C	A	P	R	I	A	R		N	
I	B	I	Z	A	R	S		I	R
L	S		D	I		I		R	O
Y	U		I	C		A		O	T
	R		N	A				N	N
	P		I						A
	Y	M	A	L	T	A	A		S
	C	R	E	T	E				S

Page 16

Coloring activity—does not require answer

Page 17

Page 18

O	K	T	O	B	E	R	F	E	S	T	
H								O	C		
A	H	A	L	L	O	W	E	E	N	H	
N	E	W	Y	E	A	R		D	G	R	
U							I	K	I		
K	Y	I	P	E	N	G		W	R	S	
K			H				A	A	T		
A			O			L	N	M			
H					L	I		A			
L	A	T	O	M	A	T	I	N	A	S	

Page 19

Page 20

G	T	R	O	U	P	I	A	L
R								
E		G	U	A	N			
H	A	R	P	Y	E	A	G	L	E
T		M	A	C	A	W		
E			U					
G			P	O	T	O	O	
R	T	O	M	T	O	M		
R	E	H	S	I	F	G	N	I	K
T	N	I	Z	T	A	O	H	

Page 21

Page 22

1. Oak
2. Cacao
3. Baobab
4. Eucalyptus
5. Cinchona
6. Maple

Page 23

Page 24

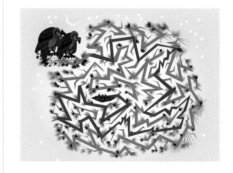

Answers

Page 25

Page 26

Page 27

1. KAKAPO
2. CASSOWARY
3. OSTRICH
4. KIWI
5. PENGUIN
6. RHEA

Page 28

E	N	I	H	R	T
K	A	I	E	T	E	U	R	I
A		T	S	G		G
I		I	S	Ł		U
R		M O		L		A	E
O		E	F	A	L	Z	N
T		S	L		E	U	W
C		O	L		G		O
I		Y	U		N		R
V	N	I	A	G	A	R	A	B

Page 29

Page 30

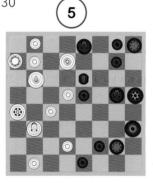

Page 31

Page 32

Page 33

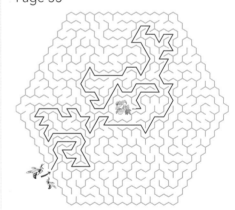

Page 34

1. Dollar - United States
2. Krone - Denmark
3. Dinar - Iraq
4. Rupee - India
5. Yen - Japan

Page 35   Wally is wearing a scarf.

Page 36

Answers

Page 37

T	R	A	V	E	L	C		M
H						I		O
E	C	O	N	C	E	R	T	S	V
A					L		U		C	H	I
T					U		B		U		O	E
E						B		S		S	W	S
R						S		S	
S	T	R	O	P	S	
				B	O	O	K	S
	C	A	R	N	I	V	A	L

Page 38

Page 39

Page 40

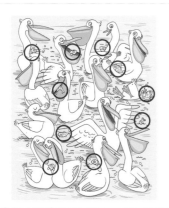

Page 41

Page 42

1. Octopus
2. Cheetah
3. Cockroach
4. Seal
5. Jellyfish
6. Zebra Fish

Page 43

Page 44

Page 45

Page 46

1. Alligator
2. Crocodile
3. Tortoise
4. Turtle
5. Chameleon
6. Gecko

Page 47

Page 48

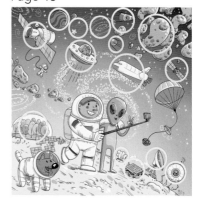

Answers

Page 49

Page 50

Page 51

1. f
2. a
3. e
4. d
5. c
6. b

Page 52

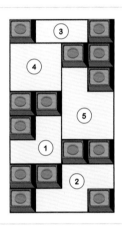

Page 53

1. (a)
2. (b)
3. (d)
4. (c)

Page 54

Page 55

Page 56

Page 57

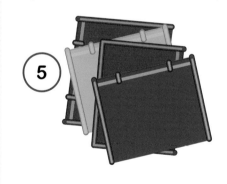

Page 58

1. e
2. c
3. a
4. b
5. d

Page 59

Page 60

1. g
2. d
3. a
4. b
5. h
6. c
7. e
8. f

Answers

Page 61

Page 62

Page 63
1. Mount Rushmore - e
2. Liberty Bell - c
3. Lincoln Memorial - a
4. Statue of Liberty - d
5. Washington Monument - b

Page 64

Page 65

Page 66

Page 67

G	O	D	L	L	U	B		N
R		A		H	U	S	K	Y	A
E	L	L						M
V	E	M						R
E	I	A						E
I	N	T		E	L	G	A	E	B
R	A	I		G				O
T	P	A		U				D
E	S	N		P	O	O	D	L	E
R	E	X	O	B			

Page 68

Page 69
1. HEDGEHOG
2. CROW
3. OWL
4. BEES
5. FOX
6. RABBIT
7. MOOSE
8. WOODPECKER
9. SQUIRREL
10. PIG

Page 70
1. c
2. f
3. a
4. b
5. d
6. e

Page 71

Build Your Own Puzzles!

Build Your Own Puzzles!

Build Your Own Puzzles!

Build Your Own Puzzles!

Build Your Own Puzzles!